3

SHINY AND HER WARDROBE OF VIRTUES

CONFIDENCE

A BELIEF IN ONESELF

BY

Sukanya Shah

First published by Birch Books 2020

ISBN - 978-81-949495-7-2

Email : books.birch@gmail.com

To Adyana.
My first. My all.
May you always be more.

From the Author's Desk

Cossetted in our homes during the thick of the Covid-19 pandemic, I made every effort to keep my toddler happy and engaged. It made me wonder about the true legacy in learning that my child will bequeath. I cannot wait to pass on this treasure of a less than perfect world to her… one that will astonish her most often, teach her most definitely and hold her to two constants—challenge and change.

Shiny And Her Wardrobe Of Virtues was born of this sentiment. Shiny is a spritely little girl who owns a magical wardrobe, with virtuous items that on adorning, change her world view…virtues that go beyond the classroom and make her feel happy and whole.

I enjoyed writing these stories of gratitude, kindness, confidence, patience and love…but more so, I enjoyed diving into these most beautiful emotions and feelings with my child.

I hope you do too.

Love,
Sukanya.

A wonderful evening at ballet class,
Shiny learned the steps rather fast.

Her ballet slippers were satiny and pink,
It made her eager, it helped her think.

"Let's try some grand jetés", said Madame
Jem,
Shiny nervously tugged at her tutu hem.

"Grand jetés are leaps, seamless splits in the air,
Spring off like a bird, go fly without a care."

"But I am so little", thought Shiny in her mind,
She broke a sweat and took one step behind.

All the big girls lined up to have a go,
"Take off, point those feet, that's all you must know."

Maya, Veda, Lara and Arya, jetéd fast and far,
They were as lovely at leaping, as they were at the barre.

Shiny stood stunned, she felt her heart beat,
Her ballet shoes sparkled, she felt a tingle in her feet.

A sudden burst of bravery came over her,
She knew she could do this, the shoes undid her fear.

"5 - 6 - 7 - 8," Madame Jem counted Shiny in,
It was her turn to shine, to strive and to win.

"Could she get this right", thought the big girls from afar,
A few extra steps later, Shiny jetéd like a star!

Her ballet slippers were enchanted, they gave her confidence,
That feeling of belief, in one's heart and conscience.

Confidence is magic, a feeling of being sure,
It makes you brave and beautiful, with all the rest assured.

Can you do it?

Yes I can!

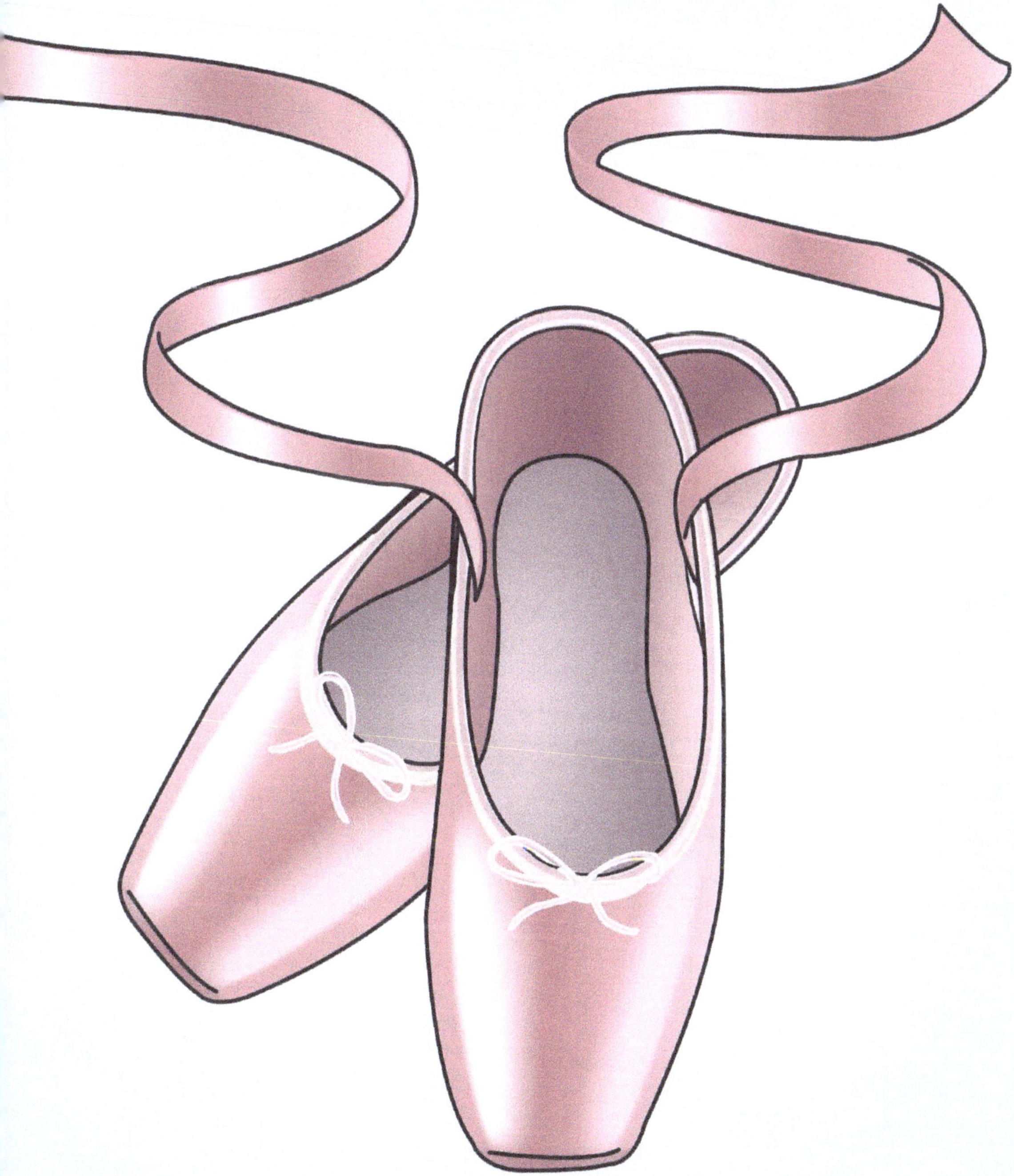

The class looked at her slippers, oh what a sight!
Shiny's dance of confidence, was a graceful delight!

She curtseyed graciously, a bow to say thank you,
She'd never forget this feeling, as her confidence grew.

Shiny took off her slippers, and felt them with her hands,
Even without them on now, her heart said "Yes you can!"

Talking points for parents:

- Talk about a new, everyday skill with your child. For example eating with chopsticks, laying the table, cycling, graduating on to a higher level puzzle, reading a book, learning a song, etc.
- Work with them through building this skill and discuss the feeling of building confidence as you go along.
- Ask them about the activities or experiences [counting, climbing, dancing] they feel confident about. Tell them what you are confident of too.
- Encourage your child to teach/help a younger child, perhaps a sibling or friend to build confidence in an activity. For example teach a little one how to use a spoon.
- When your child attempts something challenging or new, make it a sweet habit to ask them *"Can you do it?"* and have them learn the affirmative response *"Yes, I can!"*.